This Bucket List Journal Belongs To:

_____

The
Adventure
AWAITS

US National Parks by State

	Denali National Park, Alaska
	Gates of the Arctic National Park, Alaska
	Glacier Bay National Park, Alaska
	Katmai National Park, Alaska
	Kenai Fjords National Park, Alaska
	Kobuk Valley National Park, Alaska
	Lake Clark National Park, Alaska
	Wrangell-St. Elias National Park, Alaska
	National Park of American Samoa, American Samoa
	Grand Canyon National Park, Arizona
	Petrified Forest National Park, Arizona
	Saguaro National Park, Arizona
	Hot Springs National Park, Arkansas

US National Parks by State

	Channel Islands National Park, California
	Death Valley National Park, CA & NV
	Joshua Tree National Park, California
	Kings Canyon National Park, California
	Lassen Volcanic National Park, California
	Pinnacles National Park, California
	Redwood National Park, California
	Sequoia National Park, California
	Yosemite National Park, California
	Black Canyon of the Gunnison, Colorado
	Great Sand Dunes National Park, Colorado
	Mesa Verde National Park, Colorado
	Rocky Mountain National Park, Colorado
	Biscayne National Park, Florida
	Dry Tortugas National Park, Florida
	Everglades National Park, Florida

US National Parks by State

	Haleakala National Park, Hawaii
	Hawai'i Volcanoes National Park, Hawaii
	Yellowstone National Park, ID - MT - WY
	Mammoth Cave National Park, Kentucky
	Gateway Arch National Park, MO - IL
	Indiana Dunes National Park, Indiana
	Acadia National Park, Maine
	Isle Royale National Park, Michigan
	Voyageurs National Park, Minnesota
	Glacier National Park, Montana

US National Parks by State

	Great Basin National Park, Nevada
	Carlsbad Caverns National Park, NM
	Theodore Roosevelt National Park, ND
	Great Smoky Mountains, NC - TN
	Cuyahoga Valley National Park, Ohio
	Crater Lake National Park, Oregon
	Congaree National Park, South Carolina
	Badlands National Park, So Dakota
	Wind Cave National Park, So Dakota
	Big Bend National Park, Texas
	Guadalupe Mountains National Park, Texas

US National Parks by State

	Arches National Park, Utah
	Bryce Canyon National Park, Utah
	Canyonlands National Park, Utah
	Capitol Reef National Park, Utah
	Zion National Park, Utah
	Virgin Islands National Park, Virgin Islands
	Shenandoah National Park, Virginia
	Mount Rainier National Park, Washington
	North Cascades National Park, Washington
	Olympic National Park, Washington
	Grand Teton National Park, Wyoming

My National Park Bucket List in Priority Order

My National Park Bucket List in Priority Order

Park Visit # _____ Date _____

National Park
City _____ **State** _____

Went With _____ Initial Impression _____

_____ _____

Weather _____ Length of Stay _____

_____ _____

Experiences/Observations

Favorite Moment _____

_____

Wildlife Scenery Observed

_____

_____

_____

_____

Park Rating 0/10   1   2   3   4   5   6   7   8   9   10

Yes   No

Will I Visit Again?   ☐   ☐

Hiking Trail: _____

Location: _____

Date: _____ Distance_____

Companions: _____

Weather

Temperature:_____

Trail Difficulty

1   2   3   4   5

Thoughts About This Hike

_____
_____
_____
_____
_____
_____
_____
_____

Overall Rating ☆ ☆ ☆ ☆ ☆

Hiking Trail: _____

Location: _____

Date: _____ Distance_____

Companions: _____

Weather

Temperature:_____

Trail Difficulty

1   2   3   4   5

Thoughts About This Hike

_____
_____
_____
_____
_____
_____
_____
_____
_____

Overall Rating ☆ ☆ ☆ ☆ ☆

Hiking Trail: _____

Location: _____

Date: _____ Distance_____

Companions: _____

Weather

Temperature:_____

Trail Difficulty

1   2   3   4   5

Thoughts About This Hike

_____
_____
_____
_____
_____
_____
_____
_____

Overall Rating ☆ ☆ ☆ ☆ ☆

Notes – Memories - Photos

Souvenirs Ticket Stubs Maps More Pics

Park Visit # _____ Date _____

National Park
City _____ **State** _____

Went With _____ Initial Impression _____

Weather _____ Length of Stay _____

Experiences/Observations

Favorite Moment _____

_____

Wildlife Scenery Observed

_____

_____

_____

_____

Park Rating 0/10   1 2 3 4 5 6 7 8 9 10

Will I Visit Again?   Yes [ ]   No [ ]

Hiking Trail: _____

Location: _____

Date: _____ Distance_____

Companions: _____

Weather

Temperature:_____

Trail Difficulty

1   2   3   4   5

Thoughts About This Hike

_____
_____
_____
_____
_____
_____
_____
_____

Overall Rating ☆ ☆ ☆ ☆ ☆

Hiking Trail: _____

Location: _____

Date: _____ Distance_____

Companions: _____

Weather

Temperature:_____

☀ ⛅ ☁ 🌧

Trail Difficulty

1 2 3 4 5

Thoughts About This Hike

_____
_____
_____
_____
_____
_____
_____
_____

Overall Rating ☆ ☆ ☆ ☆ ☆

Hiking Trail: _____

Location: _____

Date: _____ Distance_____

Companions: _____

Weather

Temperature:_____

Trail Difficulty

1   2   3   4   5

Thoughts About This Hike

_____
_____
_____
_____
_____
_____
_____
_____

Overall Rating ☆ ☆ ☆ ☆ ☆

Notes – Memories - Photos

Souvenirs Ticket Stubs Maps More Pics

Park Visit # _____ Date _____

National Park
City _____ **State** _____

Went With _____ Initial Impression _____

Weather _____ Length of Stay _____

Experiences/Observations

Favorite Moment _____

Wildlife Scenery Observed

_____
_____
_____
_____

Park Rating 0/10   1 2 3 4 5 6 7 8 9 10

Will I Visit Again?   Yes ☐   No ☐

Hiking Trail: _____

Location: _____

Date: _____ Distance_____

Companions: _____

Weather

Temperature:_____

Trail Difficulty

1   2   3   4   5

Thoughts About This Hike

_____
_____
_____
_____
_____
_____
_____
_____

Overall Rating ☆ ☆ ☆ ☆ ☆

Hiking Trail: _____

Location: _____

Date: _____ Distance_____

Companions: _____

Weather

Temperature:_____

Trail Difficulty

1   2   3   4   5

Thoughts About This Hike

_____
_____
_____
_____
_____
_____
_____
_____

Overall Rating ☆ ☆ ☆ ☆ ☆

Hiking Trail: _____

Location: _____

Date: _____ Distance_____

Companions: _____

Weather

Temperature:_____

Trail Difficulty

1   2   3   4   5

Thoughts About This Hike

_____
_____
_____
_____
_____
_____
_____
_____

Overall Rating ☆ ☆ ☆ ☆ ☆

Notes – Memories - Photos

Souvenirs Ticket Stubs Maps More Pics

Park Visit # _____ Date _____

National Park
City _____ **State** _____

Went With _____ Initial Impression _____

Weather _____ Length of Stay _____

Experiences/Observations

Favorite Moment _____

Wildlife Scenery Observed

_____

_____

_____

_____

Park Rating 0/10   1 2 3 4 5 6 7 8 9 10

Will I Visit Again?   Yes ☐   No ☐

Hiking Trail: _____

Location: _____

Date: _____ Distance_____

Companions: _____

Weather

Temperature:_____

Trail Difficulty

1   2   3   4   5

Thoughts About This Hike

_____
_____
_____
_____
_____
_____
_____
_____

Overall Rating ☆ ☆ ☆ ☆ ☆

Hiking Trail: _____

Location: _____

Date: _____ Distance_____

Companions: _____

Weather

Temperature:_____

Trail Difficulty

1   2   3   4   5

Thoughts About This Hike

_____
_____
_____
_____
_____
_____
_____
_____

Overall Rating ☆ ☆ ☆ ☆ ☆

Hiking Trail: _____

Location: _____

Date: _____ Distance_____

Companions: _____

Weather

Temperature:_____

Trail Difficulty

1   2   3   4   5

Thoughts About This Hike

_____
_____
_____
_____
_____
_____
_____
_____

Overall Rating ☆ ☆ ☆ ☆ ☆

Notes – Memories - Photos

Souvenirs Ticket Stubs Maps More Pics

Park Visit # _____ Date _____

National Park
City   **State**

Went With _____   Initial Impression _____

_____   _____

Weather _____   Length of Stay _____

_____   _____

Experiences/Observations

Favorite Moment _____

_____

Wildlife Scenery Observed

_____

_____

_____

_____

_____

Park Rating 0/10   1 2 3 4 5 6 7 8 9 10

Will I Visit Again?   Yes [ ]   No [ ]

Hiking Trail: _____

Location: _____

Date: _____ Distance_____

Companions: _____

Weather

Temperature:_____

Trail Difficulty

1   2   3   4   5

Thoughts About This Hike

_____
_____
_____
_____
_____
_____
_____
_____

Overall Rating ☆ ☆ ☆ ☆ ☆

Hiking Trail: _____

Location: _____

Date: _____ Distance_____

Companions: _____

Weather

Temperature:_____

Trail Difficulty

1   2   3   4   5

Thoughts About This Hike

_____
_____
_____
_____
_____
_____
_____
_____

Overall Rating ☆ ☆ ☆ ☆ ☆

Hiking Trail: _____

Location: _____

Date: _____ Distance_____

Companions: _____

Weather

Temperature:_____

Trail Difficulty

1   2   3   4   5

Thoughts About This Hike

_____
_____
_____
_____
_____
_____
_____
_____

Overall Rating   ☆ ☆ ☆ ☆ ☆

Notes – Memories - Photos

Souvenirs Ticket Stubs Maps More Pics

Park Visit # _____ Date _____

National Park _____
City _____ **State** _____

Went With _____   Initial Impression _____

_____   _____

Weather _____   Length of Stay _____

_____   _____

Experiences/Observations

Favorite Moment _____

_____

Wildlife Scenery Observed

_____

_____

_____

_____

Park Rating 0/10   1 2 3 4 5 6 7 8 9 10

Will I Visit Again?   Yes ☐   No ☐

Hiking Trail: _____

Location: _____

Date: _____ Distance_____

Companions: _____

Weather

Temperature:_____

Trail Difficulty

1   2   3   4   5

Thoughts About This Hike

_____
_____
_____
_____
_____
_____
_____
_____

Overall Rating ☆ ☆ ☆ ☆ ☆

Hiking Trail: _____

Location: _____

Date: _____ Distance_____

Companions: _____

Weather

Temperature:_____

Trail Difficulty

1   2   3   4   5

Thoughts About This Hike

_____
_____
_____
_____
_____
_____
_____
_____

Overall Rating ☆ ☆ ☆ ☆ ☆

Hiking Trail: _____

Location: _____

Date: _____ Distance_____

Companions: _____

Weather

Temperature:_____

Trail Difficulty

1   2   3   4   5

Thoughts About This Hike

_____
_____
_____
_____
_____
_____
_____
_____

Overall Rating ☆ ☆ ☆ ☆ ☆

Notes – Memories - Photos

Souvenirs Ticket Stubs Maps More Pics

Park Visit # _____ Date _____

National Park
City _____ **State** _____

Went With _____ Initial Impression _____

Weather _____ Length of Stay _____

Experiences/Observations

Favorite Moment _____

_____

Wildlife Scenery Observed

_____

_____

_____

_____

Park Rating 0/10   1 2 3 4 5 6 7 8 9 10

Will I Visit Again?   Yes [ ]   No [ ]

Hiking Trail: _____

Location: _____

Date: _____ Distance_____

Companions: _____

Weather

Temperature:_____

Trail Difficulty

1   2   3   4   5

Thoughts About This Hike

_____

_____

_____

_____

_____

_____

_____

_____

Overall Rating ☆ ☆ ☆ ☆ ☆

Hiking Trail: _____

Location: _____

Date: _____ Distance_____

Companions: _____

Weather

Temperature:_____

Trail Difficulty

1   2   3   4   5

Thoughts About This Hike

_____
_____
_____
_____
_____
_____
_____
_____

Overall Rating ☆ ☆ ☆ ☆ ☆

Hiking Trail: _____

Location: _____

Date: _____ Distance_____

Companions: _____

Weather

Temperature:_____

Trail Difficulty

1   2   3   4   5

Thoughts About This Hike

_____
_____
_____
_____
_____
_____
_____
_____

Overall Rating ☆ ☆ ☆ ☆ ☆

Notes – Memories - Photos

Souvenirs Ticket Stubs Maps More Pics

Park Visit # _____ Date _____

National Park
City _____ **State** _____

Went With _____ Initial Impression _____

_____ _____

Weather _____ Length of Stay _____

_____ _____

Experiences/Observations

Favorite Moment _____

_____

Wildlife Scenery Observed

_____

_____

_____

_____

_____

Park Rating 0/10   1   2   3   4   5   6   7   8   9   10

Will I Visit Again?   Yes ☐   No ☐

Hiking Trail: _____

Location: _____

Date: _____ Distance_____

Companions: _____

Weather

Temperature:_____

Trail Difficulty

1   2   3   4   5

Thoughts About This Hike

_____
_____
_____
_____
_____
_____
_____
_____

Overall Rating   ☆ ☆ ☆ ☆ ☆

Hiking Trail: _____

Location: _____

Date: _____   Distance_____

Companions: _____

Weather

Temperature:_____

Trail Difficulty

1   2   3   4   5

Thoughts About This Hike

_____
_____
_____
_____
_____
_____
_____
_____

Overall Rating ☆ ☆ ☆ ☆ ☆

Hiking Trail: _____

Location: _____

Date: _____ Distance_____

Companions: _____

Weather

Temperature:_____

Trail Difficulty

1   2   3   4   5

Thoughts About This Hike

_____
_____
_____
_____
_____
_____
_____
_____

Overall Rating ☆ ☆ ☆ ☆ ☆

Notes – Memories - Photos

Souvenirs Ticket Stubs Maps More Pics

Park Visit # _____ Date _____

National Park
City   **State**

Went With _____   Initial Impression _____

_____   _____

Weather _____   Length of Stay _____

_____   _____

Experiences/Observations

Favorite Moment _____

_____

Wildlife Scenery Observed

_____

_____

_____

_____

Park Rating 0/10   1 2 3 4 5 6 7 8 9 10

Will I Visit Again?   Yes [ ]   No [ ]

Hiking Trail: _____

Location: _____

Date: _____ Distance_____

Companions: _____

Weather

Temperature:_____

Trail Difficulty

1   2   3   4   5

Thoughts About This Hike

_____
_____
_____
_____
_____
_____
_____
_____

Overall Rating ☆ ☆ ☆ ☆ ☆

Hiking Trail: _____

Location: _____

Date: _____ Distance_____

Companions: _____

Weather

Temperature:_____

Trail Difficulty

1   2   3   4   5

Thoughts About This Hike

_____
_____
_____
_____
_____
_____
_____
_____

Overall Rating ☆ ☆ ☆ ☆ ☆

Hiking Trail: _____

Location: _____

Date: _____ Distance_____

Companions: _____

Weather

Temperature:_____

Trail Difficulty

1   2   3   4   5

Thoughts About This Hike

_____
_____
_____
_____
_____
_____
_____
_____

Overall Rating ☆ ☆ ☆ ☆ ☆

Notes – Memories - Photos

Souvenirs Ticket Stubs Maps More Pics

Park Visit # _____ Date _____

National Park
City **State**

Went With _____ Initial Impression _____

_____ _____

Weather _____ Length of Stay _____

_____ _____

Experiences/Observations

Favorite Moment _____

_____

Wildlife Scenery Observed

_____

_____

_____

_____

_____

Park Rating 0/10   1 2 3 4 5 6 7 8 9 10

Will I Visit Again?   Yes [ ]   No [ ]

Hiking Trail: _____

Location: _____

Date: _____ Distance_____

Companions: _____

Weather

Temperature:_____

Trail Difficulty

1   2   3   4   5

Thoughts About This Hike

_____
_____
_____
_____
_____
_____
_____
_____

Overall Rating   ☆ ☆ ☆ ☆ ☆

Hiking Trail: _____

Location: _____

Date: _____ Distance_____

Companions: _____

Weather

Temperature:_____

Trail Difficulty

1   2   3   4   5

Thoughts About This Hike

_____
_____
_____
_____
_____
_____
_____
_____

Overall Rating ☆ ☆ ☆ ☆ ☆

Hiking Trail: _____

Location: _____

Date: _____ Distance_____

Companions: _____

Weather

Temperature:_____

☀ ⛅ ☁ 🌧

Trail Difficulty

1   2   3   4   5

Thoughts About This Hike

_____
_____
_____
_____
_____
_____
_____
_____

Overall Rating ☆ ☆ ☆ ☆ ☆

Notes – Memories - Photos

Souvenirs Ticket Stubs Maps More Pics

Park Visit # _____ Date _____

National Park
City   **State**

Went With _____

Initial Impression _____

Weather _____

Length of Stay _____

Experiences/Observations

Favorite Moment _____

_____

Wildlife Scenery Observed

_____

_____

_____

_____

_____

Park Rating 0/10   1   2   3   4   5   6   7   8   9   10

Will I Visit Again?   Yes ☐   No ☐

Hiking Trail: _____

Location: _____

Date: _____   Distance_____

Companions: _____

Weather

Temperature:_____

Trail Difficulty

1   2   3   4   5

Thoughts About This Hike

_____

_____

_____

_____

_____

_____

_____

_____

Overall Rating ☆ ☆ ☆ ☆ ☆

Hiking Trail: _____

Location: _____

Date: _____ Distance_____

Companions: _____

Weather

Temperature:_____

Trail Difficulty

1   2   3   4   5

Thoughts About This Hike

_____
_____
_____
_____
_____
_____
_____
_____

Overall Rating ☆ ☆ ☆ ☆ ☆

Hiking Trail: _____

Location: _____

Date: _____   Distance_____

Companions: _____

Weather

Temperature:_____

Trail Difficulty

1   2   3   4   5

Thoughts About This Hike

_____
_____
_____
_____
_____
_____
_____
_____
_____

Overall Rating ☆ ☆ ☆ ☆ ☆

Notes – Memories - Photos

Souvenirs Ticket Stubs Maps More Pics

Park Visit # _____ Date _____

National Park
City _____ **State** _____

Went With _____ Initial Impression _____

_____ _____

Weather _____ Length of Stay _____

_____ _____

Experiences/Observations

Favorite Moment _____

_____

Wildlife Scenery Observed

_____

_____

_____

_____

_____

Park Rating 0/10   1 2 3 4 5 6 7 8 9 10

Will I Visit Again?   Yes [ ]   No [ ]

Hiking Trail: _____

Location: _____

Date: _____ Distance_____

Companions: _____

Weather

Temperature:_____

Trail Difficulty

1   2   3   4   5

Thoughts About This Hike

_____

_____

_____

_____

_____

_____

_____

_____

Overall Rating ☆ ☆ ☆ ☆ ☆

Hiking Trail: _____

Location: _____

Date: _____ Distance_____

Companions: _____

Weather

Temperature:_____

Trail Difficulty

1   2   3   4   5

Thoughts About This Hike

_____
_____
_____
_____
_____
_____
_____
_____

Overall Rating   ☆ ☆ ☆ ☆ ☆

Hiking Trail: _____

Location: _____

Date: _____ Distance_____

Companions: _____

Weather

Temperature:_____

Trail Difficulty

1   2   3   4   5

Thoughts About This Hike

_____
_____
_____
_____
_____
_____
_____
_____

Overall Rating ☆ ☆ ☆ ☆ ☆

Notes – Memories - Photos

Souvenirs Ticket Stubs Maps More Pics

Park Visit # _____ Date _____

National Park
City   **State**

Went With   Initial Impression

Weather   Length of Stay

Experiences/Observations

Favorite Moment

            Wildlife Scenery Observed

Park Rating 0/10   1 2 3 4 5 6 7 8 9 10

                     Yes   No

Will I Visit Again?   [ ]   [ ]

Hiking Trail: _____

Location: _____

Date: _____ Distance_____

Companions: _____

Weather

Temperature:_____

Trail Difficulty

1   2   3   4   5

Thoughts About This Hike

_____
_____
_____
_____
_____
_____
_____
_____

Overall Rating ☆ ☆ ☆ ☆ ☆

Hiking Trail: _____

Location: _____

Date: _____ Distance_____

Companions: _____

Weather

Temperature:_____

Trail Difficulty

1   2   3   4   5

Thoughts About This Hike

_____
_____
_____
_____
_____
_____
_____
_____

Overall Rating ☆ ☆ ☆ ☆ ☆

Hiking Trail: _____

Location: _____

Date: _____ Distance_____

Companions: _____

Weather

Temperature:_____

Trail Difficulty

1   2   3   4   5

Thoughts About This Hike

_____
_____
_____
_____
_____
_____
_____
_____

Overall Rating ☆ ☆ ☆ ☆ ☆

Notes – Memories - Photos

Souvenirs Ticket Stubs Maps More Pics

Park Visit # _____ Date _____

National Park
City _____ **State** _____

Went With _____ Initial Impression _____

_____ _____

Weather _____ Length of Stay _____

_____ _____

Experiences/Observations

Favorite Moment _____

_____

Wildlife Scenery Observed

_____

_____

_____

_____

Park Rating 0/10   1 2 3 4 5 6 7 8 9 10

Will I Visit Again?   Yes [ ]   No [ ]

Hiking Trail: _____

Location: _____

Date: _____ Distance_____

Companions: _____

Weather

Temperature:_____

Trail Difficulty

1   2   3   4   5

Thoughts About This Hike

_____
_____
_____
_____
_____
_____
_____
_____

Overall Rating ☆ ☆ ☆ ☆ ☆

Hiking Trail: _____

Location: _____

Date: _____ Distance_____

Companions: _____

Weather

Temperature:_____

Trail Difficulty

1   2   3   4   5

Thoughts About This Hike

_____
_____
_____
_____
_____
_____
_____
_____

Overall Rating ☆ ☆ ☆ ☆ ☆

Hiking Trail: _____

Location: _____

Date: _____ Distance_____

Companions: _____

Weather

Temperature:_____

Trail Difficulty

1   2   3   4   5

Thoughts About This Hike

_____
_____
_____
_____
_____
_____
_____
_____

Overall Rating ☆ ☆ ☆ ☆ ☆

Notes – Memories - Photos

Souvenirs Ticket Stubs Maps More Pics

Park Visit # _____ Date _____

National Park
City _____ **State** _____

Went With _____ Initial Impression _____

Weather _____ Length of Stay _____

Experiences/Observations

Favorite Moment _____

_____

Wildlife Scenery Observed

_____

_____

_____

_____

Park Rating 0/10   1 2 3 4 5 6 7 8 9 10

Will I Visit Again?   Yes ☐   No ☐

Hiking Trail: _____

Location: _____

Date: _____ Distance_____

Companions: _____

Weather

Temperature:_____

Trail Difficulty

1   2   3   4   5

Thoughts About This Hike

_____
_____
_____
_____
_____
_____
_____
_____

Overall Rating ☆ ☆ ☆ ☆ ☆

Hiking Trail: _____

Location: _____

Date: _____   Distance_____

Companions: _____

Weather

Temperature:_____

Trail Difficulty

1   2   3   4   5

Thoughts About This Hike

_____
_____
_____
_____
_____
_____
_____
_____
_____

Overall Rating ☆ ☆ ☆ ☆ ☆

Hiking Trail: _____

Location: _____

Date: _____ Distance_____

Companions: _____

Weather

Temperature:_____

Trail Difficulty

1 2 3 4 5

Thoughts About This Hike

_____
_____
_____
_____
_____
_____
_____
_____

Overall Rating ☆ ☆ ☆ ☆ ☆

Notes – Memories - Photos

Souvenirs Ticket Stubs Maps More Pics

Park Visit # _____ Date _____

National Park
City   **State**

Went With _____   Initial Impression _____

Weather _____   Length of Stay _____

Experiences/Observations

Favorite Moment _____

        Wildlife Scenery Observed

_____

_____

_____

_____

Park Rating 0/10   1   2   3   4   5   6   7   8   9   10

                              Yes   No

Will I Visit Again?   ☐   ☐

Hiking Trail: _____

Location: _____

Date: _____ Distance_____

Companions: _____

Weather

Temperature:_____

Trail Difficulty

1   2   3   4   5

Thoughts About This Hike

_____
_____
_____
_____
_____
_____
_____
_____

Overall Rating ☆ ☆ ☆ ☆ ☆

Hiking Trail: _____

Location: _____

Date: _____   Distance_____

Companions: _____

Weather

Temperature:_____

Trail Difficulty

1   2   3   4   5

Thoughts About This Hike

_____
_____
_____
_____
_____
_____
_____
_____

Overall Rating   ☆ ☆ ☆ ☆ ☆

Hiking Trail: _____

Location: _____

Date: _____ Distance_____

Companions: _____

Weather

Temperature:_____

Trail Difficulty

1   2   3   4   5

Thoughts About This Hike

_____
_____
_____
_____
_____
_____
_____
_____

Overall Rating ☆ ☆ ☆ ☆ ☆

Notes – Memories - Photos

Souvenirs Ticket Stubs Maps More Pics

Time to head back to
Amazon to order another
book. If you enjoyed this
bucket list book,
we hope you will share
your opinion by leaving
a review on Amazon.
Thank you,
Bucket List Publishers

CPSIA information can be obtained
at www.ICGtesting.com
Printed in the USA
LVHW081447261020
669836LV00015BA/901